Whispers in the Wind

Biblical Poems

EDNA ANDERSON COOPER

Inspired and Endorsed by the Holy Spirit

WestBow Press books may be ordered through booksellers or by contacting:

WestBow Press
A Division of Thomas Nelson & Zondervan
1663 Liberty Drive
Bloomington, IN 47403
www.westbowpress.com
844-714-3454

Scripture taken from the King James Version of the Bible.

ISBN: 978-1-6642-3736-0 (sc)
ISBN: 978-1-6642-3737-7 (e)

Library of Congress Control Number: 2021912244

Print information available on the last page.

WestBow Press rev. date: 07/23/2021

WESTBOW
PRESS®
A DIVISION OF THOMAS NELSON
& ZONDERVAN

Dedication

This book of biblical poems is dedicated to my two daughters: Hayley and Haven; my son, Adam. I pray that I have given each of you love and support throughout your life. I hope that I have given each of you faith, support, and constant encouragement. The teaching that you received is to always believe in yourself, your dreams and most important God. I want each of you to remember me as the strongest person you know. I want to thank my family also!

The thing that makes you sleepy is the thing you should pay attention to!

Contents

Man

You were made from nothing,
But you became something—
Taken from the earth's residue.
No other creation has made such a breakthrough.
God's breath made you a living soul;
You were part of God's precious goal.
God decided it is not good for you to be alone,
So He made woman from your bone.
You had dominion over the earth;
Because of sin, God gave you a spiritual rebirth.
What a divine wonder you became!
Because of your disobedience, everything changed.
Deep compassion for you will never be forsaken;
The love of God is yours for the taking.
The Father, Son, and Holy Spirit had made the plan.
They helped create a magnificent man!

Woman

Taken from the rib of man
Before time, you were part of God's plan.
Everything in the garden belonged to you;
It was so perfect, like the morning dew.
The serpent was clever and very wise
Because he knew the unfolding of your eyes.
Had you not listened in the garden,
Then your life would not have been pardoned.
Pain and suffering you shall endure;
It is part of God's plan, and it is for sure.
You are glorious and magnificent being,
And we know man will not be disagreeing!

Adam and Eve

Who is to blame,
Adam or Eve?
It would have been wonderful
If only they had believed!
The Lord gave Adam the commandment
Not to eat of the fruit.
His curiosity got the best of him,
So he went in pursuit.

The devil beguiled Eve to think
that she would not die.
Persuasion was easy—she could not deny!
She could have indulged in the fruit
all day long.
She could have even made a fruitcake
while singing a song.

The devil was clever, even quite stunning;
His tricks and lies were so cunning.
Adam could have said no at the beginning,
But instead he chose death as his ending.

Humankind now pays for the sin of Adam.
I wish down in my heart that it had not happened.
We must go on day by day
Because Jesus Christ has made a way.

He left us a comforter, the Holy Spirit,
To lead, guide, and protect us.
The kingdom we will inherit!

I do not know why Adam chose the author of pain.
Since that day humanity has not been the same!

Night with the Frogs

"Pharaoh, let my people go."
It was so easy—don't you know?

Moses warned you what would happen;
You disregarded, and the land of Egypt was blackened!

Croaking and hopping, they were your guests.
The Egyptians could not get any rest!

They overtook the water, food, river, and beds.
If only you had been obedient, they would have fled.

Because of your refusal, God hardened your heart.
You were defeated at the start!

"Pharaoh, let my people go."
Only from God will goodness flow!

The Red Sea

"Moses, lift thy rod and stretch out thy hand."
The Red Sea will obey at the Lord's command.

The great water was divided;
Peace and refuge the Lord provided.

And the water formed a great wall,
Its beauty cascading like a waterfall.

The Israelites passed safely through the Red Sea;
Released from bondage, they were free!

And Israel saw the great work of the Lord.
Witnessing His power will not be ignored!

The Flood

It's gonna rain; it's gonna rain.
It was not easy for Noah to explain.

The sun continued to shine so bright;
The forecast showed no rain in sight.

God gave instructions to Noah to build the ark;
Building it with gopher wood was just the start.

Carefully gather all living creatures in pairs.
Lead and guide them with special care.

When it began to rain, it began to pour.
Grief and humanity would be no more.

God commanded Noah to shut the door;
The ark began to float away from the shore.

The water began to rise—oh so high.
A miracle was happening; you could not deny!

The people were screaming and crying because of their sin.
Noah said, "Too late—God has the key, and you cannot get in."

It rained for forty days and forty nights.
Noah and his family were waiting for the first sunlight.

Never again would the earth be destroyed by water.
The rainbow in the sky is the promise from our Heavenly Father!

Rainbow

A reflection of colors from the sun's rays
Always helps the world in dismay.
It was a promise made by God.
Its beauty lights up the sky like a lightning rod.
He splashed the colors like a work of art;
Each detail was made from God's loving heart.
Purple, red, orange, yellow, green, indigo, violet, and blue—
The vision is always refreshing, like the morning dew.
The raindrops give an important start.
His love for humankind will never be torn apart!

Mary

Mary had a little lamb,
A descendant of Abraham.

Although she was a virgin,
The task at hand was urgent.

Mary, Mary, was chosen from among many,
Not even at the age of twenty.

Poised and dainty, quite a lady,
She was filled with the Holy Spirit—
many thought she was crazy!

Mary, Mary, did not complain
or say a mumbling word.
Her reputation and name might be slurred.

Mary was faithful and true to the end.
The baby she carried became everyone's friend!

8

Star

I wish I could touch just one star.

Maybe not, because heaven is far.

If I could climb just one starlit stair,

I would not live life in despair.

There is a purpose for me in heaven.

The biblical number is seven.

God will release me from the depression.

Nothing shall prosper—not one weapon.

Twinkle, twinkle, how I love you so,

Because you are the light that shone for Jesus long ago!

Like a diamond, you shine so bright.

You cover the darkness with your light!

The Dogwood

What an impressive tree!
It was used to save me.

Its trunk and branches were strongly built.
For shame and torture, it was used with no guilt.

Its wood was used to construct a cross
For rescuing humankind—no one would be lost.

Smothered with white blossoms and stained with red,
Petals contoured into a cross to represent how my Christ bled.

Enjoy her beauty only in the spring,
Anticipating Easter to celebrate the King.

Thousands of years have passed and gone,
But the impressive tree will forever be known!

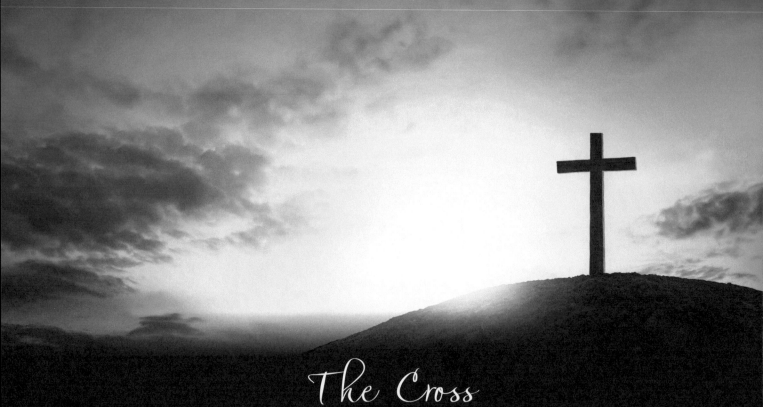

The Cross

Two planks of wood crisscrossed and nailed together,
Used for punishment to remember.

Upon the hill it stands—
A death sentence subjected to man.

Oh, how it was used to crucify my Jesus;
It was full of arrogance, even though He was blameless.

It murdered my Jesus between two thieves;
All who looked upon Him began to grieve.

It is a symbol of suffering and shame,
Known in history of great fame.

Because it could not rectify,
Never again will it be used to crucify!

Jesus

J—Justification on the cross.

E—Example of love on the cross.

S—Surrender all on the cross.

U—Unconditional love on the cross.

S—Separation on the cross.

Because of the cross, no one is lost!

Rock with Jesus

Rockabye baby, in Jesus's arms—
Safe in His refuge, you will come to no harm.
When the day breaks,
Jesus does not sleep; He is still awake.
When you are up against a mountain,
Jesus will not let you fall.
He will lead, protect, and guide you;
Jesus will be your all!

(sing to the tune "Rock-a-Bye Baby")

A Place Called Heaven

A spectacular place—the home of God and His angels,
Where the saved go to live after death
and will know no strangers.

There will be supreme happiness and bliss;
Trials and tribulations on earth will not be missed.

There is nothing but joy and peace up there;
Holiness and worshipping are everywhere!

A place of great beauty and pleasure,
Feeling the presence of God without measure.

The streets are paved with gold—
Just the beginning of how the story will be told.

The walls are decorated with precious stone;
Jesus sits at the right hand of God's throne.

Sun and moon will not shine;
The glory of God will be divine.

In this place there are many mansions.
Jesus hung on the cross; He paid the ransom.

This place is filled with joy and reward.
There is no more death, sorrow, or tears to record.

Way up high in the sky,
Where we will sing the great by-and-by!

A Place Called Hell

It's full of dark chambers with no light.
The soul is tormented day and night.

Satan is the master; he rules the place.
Because of arrogance, he fell from grace.

The wicked are bound and restrained with chains,
Mourning, groaning, and enduring such pain.

Sinner and unbeliever spend eternity after death
Praying every second to take the last breath.

The flame and heat are so intense.
Having faith and belief is exercising common sense!

There will be weeping and gnashing of teeth.
Every day the body will experience great grief.

This is a place where the spirits of the dead live.
There is no compassion or sympathy to give.

The fire was kindled in God's anger.
The wicked perished in great danger.

Hell and destruction are never full—
It's an eternal residence for the fool!

My Mansion

I have a mansion in glory.
There I can walk and tell the story.

The structure is beautifully made, not by hand—
Pillars erected, all so grand.

I do not know its color;
It is a mystery I will discover.

I do not know its size;
The magnificence will amaze my eyes!

The staircase is embellished with gold;
Half of the story has not been told.

I know one of them belongs to me;
There life will be safe and carefree.

Jesus went away to prepare a place for me.
Heaven is where my mansion will be!

Job

He gave reverence daily to God,
His faithfulness as strong as a rod.

He was a perfectly upright man,
One who eschewed evil and followed God's plan.

God recommended him to the devil;
He was a true servant on God's highest level.

He lost everything that he had—substance, children, and wife—
Yet he still praised God in all his strife.

Satan smote him with sore boils;
He used ashes for comfort instead of oil.

Satan tried hard to destroy him without cause.
Because he held to his integrity, he received applause.

For seven days and nights, his grief was very great.
His foolish speaking wife he would not debate.

God giveth, and He taketh away.
Still Job did not go astray.

He remained trustworthy and loyal.
He had comfort in knowing he defeated the destroyer.

Seasons

Winter is a season that releases an arctic breath of air;
Every living creature lives in solitaire.

Spring is a season full of flowers;
Nature comes to life to demonstrate its power.

Summer is the season where everything comes to maturity,
Embracing the physical world in tight security.

Fall is a season that establishes its glory;
The avid colors—red, orange, and brown—tell the story.

To everything there is a season;
It is hard to comprehend God's creation beyond reason!

Snow

What can wash me white as snow?
Nothing but the blood of Jesus—don't you know?

The beauty of your whiteness layers the ground;
Each flake that falls is so profound.

You cover the ground like a big celebration;
All look upon you in great admiration.

The purity puts forth a lovely presentation,
Because you are the topic of every conversation.

Icicles decorate from your condensation,
Preparing for God's great coronation.

The white flakes floating in the atmosphere
Let you know that Jesus is near!

Storms

Storms come and go,
Surrounding the earth, going to and fro.

Going from west to east,
Your behavior is like a beast.

Lightning is a flash of electricity;
No darkness can hide your visibility.

Thunder interrupts the silence of the sky.
Jesus is standing nearby.

Rain pours forcefully from the clouds;
Each droplet is released to freedom, all so proud.

Large chunks of ice rain down on the earth,
Causing havoc for all they are worth.

Strong winds are allowed to become a twister.
We're longing to hear God's voice, just a whisper!

God's Voice

His voice sounds like music to my ears,
Dancing clouds releasing drops of tears.

The sound of thunder makes me realize He is near;
I'm wrapped in peace and have no fear.

Everything moves at His command;
The sun, stars, and moon obey on demand.

Your powerful wonders linger above;
Your majesty is touched with much love.

We share the land, water, and air; do not be in despair.
It is wonderful to know He gives you special care.

He gently says, "Hush, my dear.
My arms are your protection; be of good cheer!"

Your vibration echoes deep in the valley,
Waiting patiently for the grand finale!

Is He There?

There is a path with no directions.
There is a road that has no intersections.
There is a street that has no crossing.
There is a highway that has no stopping.
There is a bridge that you cannot cross over.
There is a railroad that has no pass over.
There is a mountain that cannot be climbed.
There is a valley too low, where the bells do not chime.
There is an ocean so wide you cannot sail.
His hands and feet show proof of the nails.
In all the good and bad things that happen in your life,
Jesus is the answer to all of your strife.
No one can understand the heartaches
and pain that lie ahead.
Just believe Jesus is not dead.
Sure, we have faith and trust,
But what is the use if we cannot readjust?
We are told, "Do not worry; just pray."
He will always make a way.
When Mary and Martha told Jesus, "You are too late,"
Jesus replied, "Where is your faith?"
We hurt, we cry, we learn.
Jesus is there to give us the right turn.

You can see the storm approaching.
You can hear the thunder roar.
You can see the lightning flash.
You can see the raindrops fall.
Jesus is still there;
He is your all and all.
He sits high and looks low;
He knows the pain and suffering
That comes down below.
Remember, He is the first and the last.
His love for you will never be surpassed.
Through happiness, joy, sadness, and pain,
Know that victory you will attain.
You are wondering if you are going to fall.
Jesus's love for you is above all.
Another day, the sun will shine,
But no one knows the pain left behind.
The stars twinkle brightly in the night.
You are wondering if you are alone in this fight.
Upon the sea, Jesus walked calmly,
Reassuring his disciples with his voice warmly.
No matter what you are going through,
Just know that Jesus is the morning dew!

Blessings

One today,
Two tomorrow,
Three yesterday—
Every day I pray.

I will not forget what you have done.
In three days victory was won!

There were many blessings placed on the cross.
You hung, bled, and died so no one would be lost.

Blessings in the morning,
Blessings at noon,
Blessings in the evening—
All day long, blessings are happening,
Rejoicing, and receiving!

23

How I Pray

I pray tomorrow;
My heart is filled with sorrow.

I pray today;
I can see the sun's rays.

I pray tonight
With all my might.

I pray in the morning;
He will hear my groaning.

I pray at noon,
Hoping He will not return soon!

I pray in the evening,
Even though my heart is grieving.

I look to the hills,
whence cometh my help.
I pray that my prayer he will accept!

Today

Today it is raining.

I should feel sad,

But instead each raindrop makes me glad.

The drumming sound of the rain

Clearly erases my aching pain.

My teardrops roll softly down my cheek;

I am caught up in my emotions that make me feel unique.

I know tomorrow will make me feel better,

Because God has the whole world in his hand—that's what matters.

Each raindrop that falls

Reminds me that God controls everything after all.

Sunday 1

Monday 2

Tuesday 3

Wednesday 4

Thursday 5

Days 6

Friday 6

Saturday 7

Sunday, the first day I feel weak—
Immediate refuge my soul does seek.
Monday, my emotions are in constant fear.
Yesterday is gone, today is here, and
tomorrow is drawing near!
Tuesday, I smile, or maybe I cry.
I often ask the question, "Why?"
Wednesday, the pain is forever aching in my bones.
My heart beats slowly to musical tones.
Thursday, I feel the sorrow in my heart.
My dreadful feelings will not depart.
Friday is better—I hear God's voice.
Give praise—give honor! I will rejoice!
Saturday, I realize all miseries will cease,
Because this is the last day to have some peace.

Why

I do not understand why there is so much pain.
There are many trials and tribulations
for which I cannot complain.

Maybe tomorrow I will feel better.
The sorrow burns deeply like the scarlet letter.

My burning lips are rapidly becoming coarse.
My words are silent, and my voice has become hoarse.

I cannot look back or turn around.
I have to go forward; I cannot fall down!

I look to the left and to the right.
I cannot give up; I must continue to fight!

Another river I must cross—
God, help me, or I will be lost.

If I believe and have confessed,
Eventually, my soul will be at rest.

Stop Your Weeping

Weeping may endure for a night.
Do not give up; continue to fight!

But joy cometh in the morning.
Be of good cheer; stop your mourning.

In every circumstance, He will give you rest.
Hold your head up; it is only a test.

Continue to pray with all your might.
He is listening; He will be your guiding light!

When you think you are ready to quit,
Jesus will step in; your sobbing He will not permit.

Release yourself from bondage; have no fear.
Jesus will catch each falling tear.

I know you might be feeling low,
And you feel like you have nowhere to go.

Remember, you are not left alone.
In time, you will be singing a brand-new song!

He knows exactly what you are going through.
At the right time, you will see your breakthrough!

He is never late; He is always on time.
His Holy Spirit is divine.

Jesus is your precious friend;
He will be there till the end.

Mother's Day

We set aside this wonderful day
To honor you in a special way.

Even though it comes once a year,
My eyes are always filled with tears.

God took a rib from Adam to make you whole,
And that is when you became a living soul.

Mother, you are special; we all know this to be true.
God's divine touch made you fresh as morning dew.

You are like the fragrance of a bouquet of flowers;
You give your time and so many hours.

You take the time and are always humble;
You direct our paths to make sure we do not stumble.

After the rain, there comes the sun.
You spread your love like God's begotten son.

The hours of the day never end,
Because God has your back; He is your best friend.

You speak soft and gentle words that tell a story.
You shall wear a crown in glory.

If I look in the sky where the clouds are white,
They remind me of your smile so bright.

You prepare meals and take care
of us when we are sick;
You are there even though the load
gets heavy, like a brick.

Many days I know you are tired and in pain.
But day after day, you never complain.

You continue to give words that make you shine,
Because your love comes from the Divine.

You are the next best thing to God.
When you get to heaven, you will
be part of his angelic squad.

Mother, remember: this is your special day.
Smile, dance, laugh, or cry because on
this day, you can have your way!

Happy Father's Day

We sat aside this remarkable day,
To honor you in a special way.

Even though it comes once a year,
You are always there to give us a shout and a cheer.

God, the Father, the Son, and the Holy Spirit came together to discuss,
How to make a man from the residue of dust.

God gave you dominion over the earth,
You receive a complete spiritual rebirth.

Father, you are unique; we all know this to be true,
Because God's sacred touch made you an appealing statue.

You were there when we began to crawl,
Now you are standing near when we fall.

You give support throughout our life,
Because you are strong and encouraging us never to give up the fight!

WHAT DOES FATHER MEAN?
F-friend till the end
A-amazing things you do
T-tender care you give
H-how you give honor to God
E-everlasting love you share
R-righteousness thou are

Father, you are an extraordinary human being, don't you know,
You were made in his image beautiful as a rainbow!

Home

Home is where happiness begins.

Laughter, smiles, and hugs will never end.

The family gathering and food are all that matters.

The noise of pots and pans makes a loud clatter.

Dad, mom, daughter, and son,

Uncle, aunt, and cousins—so much fun.

The bright-red door is always open;

The love that is shared will never be broken.

The aroma of homemade cooking lingers in the air—

What a wonderful blessing for us to share!

Cancer

Cancer, what a dreadful word!

You are not welcome here; have you heard?

You attack my body because you cheated;

With prayers and fasting, you are defeated.

You may have won the battle but not the war,

Because my faith is strong like sand on the seashore.

No weapon formed against me shall prosper.

Jesus cleansed my sin; He is the washer.

I know the fight is not mine;

He will heal me right on time.

In the pit of hell, you should be cast;

Your pain and suffering will not last.

So buckle up, cancer; you've met your match.

This is one body you will not snatch.

Jesus is my divine healer.

My path is directed by the miraculous leader!

33

2020

In the year of 2020,
All races of people were frightened, wondering
If there would be plenty.

The coronavirus came and invaded the world;
The land, air, and water were in a whirl.

The pandemic caused many to die;
Everyone realized this was no lie.

The earth's population began to live in fear,
Wondering if Jesus's coming was near.

Unemployment rocketed sky high;
Gas prices were at their lowest.
But some still sang the great by-and-by.

Individuals wearing face masks looking like zombies,
Standing six feet apart, and nobody was happy.
Sanitized lotion left every shelf.
Are we thinking of others or only ourselves?

No school, no sports, no work, not even church—
Everything was hushed; where do we search?

God tells us if we humble ourselves and turn from
our wicked ways,
he will heal the land.
Every race, religion, and country should pull together,
because this is the answer.
This is the final plan!

The Lord's Prayer

Our Father which art in heaven,

Hallowed be thy name.

Thy kingdom come.

Thy will be done in earth, as it is in heaven.

Give us this day our daily bread.

And forgive us our debts, as we forgive our debtors.

And lead us not into temptation,

but deliver us from evil:

For thine is the kingdom,

and the power,

and the glory,

forever.

Amen.